Original title:

Rising Through Love

Author: Eliora Lumiste

ISBN HARDBACK: 978-9916-89-751-5

ISBN PAPERBACK: 978-9916-89-752-2

ISBN EBOOK: 978-9916-89-753-9

Sanctified Journeys of Togetherness

In the light of grace we tread,
Hand in hand, where faith is led.
Paths entwined in sacred trust,
We find our hope, we rise from dust.

Each step echoes love's decree,
Hearts united, we shall be free.
Through trials, our spirits soar,
Together we seek, forevermore.

Harmonies of the Beloved

Soft whispers sing from above,
Melodies of endless love.
In the silence, joy takes flight,
With each note, the soul ignites.

Together in this sacred tune,
We dance beneath the watchful moon.
Voices blended, strong and clear,
In harmony, we cast out fear.

Echoes of Sacred Commitment

Vows spoken, a promise we share,
In every heartbeat, love laid bare.
Through storms of life, we will stand,
Guided always by His hand.

The echoes of our solemn swears,
Reflect the light of answered prayers.
In unity, our spirits climb,
With faith that conquers space and time.

Celestial Blooming of Union

From seeds of dreams, our love will grow,
In fields of grace where blessings flow.
Each petal's hue, a life we weave,
In God's embrace, we dare believe.

With every dawn, new colors arise,
A tapestry beneath the skies.
Together we flourish, hand in hand,
In the garden of His promised land.

Love's Celestial Symphony

In the heavens, melodies sing,
Notes of mercy, love's offering.
Hearts entwined in divine grace,
Harmony's dance fills the space.

Strings of faith in gentle play,
Echoing joy, night and day.
Each heartbeat a sacred chime,
Resounding through the sands of time.

With every prayer, our spirits soar,
In unity, we seek and explore.
A symphony of hope reborn,
In love's embrace, we're never torn.

Light Illuminating Our Path

In shadows deep, the light shines bright,
Guiding souls through the endless night.
With every step, His love unfolds,
Casting warmth as the truth beholds.

The lantern of grace we cling to tight,
Bringing courage to face the fight.
Upon this road, our fears subside,
He walks with us, our faithful guide.

With faith's glow, we journey on,
Through valleys low and mountains drawn.
Each moment bright with His embrace,
In the glow of love, we find our place.

The Sacred Space of Hearts

In the stillness, whispers rise,
Hearts unite, a sacred prize.
In silence, where our spirits meet,
Love's essence makes us complete.

Beneath the veil of earthly bounds,
A sanctuary where grace abounds.
In every glance, a shared prayer,
A bond that breathes the holy air.

The space we share, divine and true,
Reflects the love that we pursue.
In sacred circles, hearts entwined,
A tapestry of souls aligned.

Pilgrims of a Harmonious Bond

As pilgrims roam on life's vast sea,
United in love, we journey free.
With every step, our souls embrace,
In grace, we find our rightful place.

With open hearts, we share the light,
Healing wounds from every plight.
Together, we'll break every chain,
In joy and laughter, love shall reign.

Through trials faced and battles fought,
In every lesson, wisdom sought.
As travelers of faith, hand in hand,
We walk together on sacred land.

Union of Eternal Souls

In the stillness of the night,
Two spirits dance in the light.
Bound by faith and sacred grace,
Together, they find their place.

A love that knows no decay,
Guided by the stars' soft sway.
In whispers shared, they take flight,
Eternal souls in love's warm light.

With each breath, a prayer they weave,
In every glance, they believe.
Hearts entwined, they rise above,
In unity, they rejoice in love.

The journey long, yet never lone,
In every trial, they have grown.
Their bond, a tapestry divine,
In faith and love, forever shine.

Through the storms and through the calm,
In each other, they find the balm.
Souls united, pure and true,
In this union, they are new.

Songs of Ascendant Love

From valleys low to mountains high,
Their voices soar, a sacred sigh.
In harmony, they find their grace,
A melody in time and space.

Like rivers flowing to the sea,
Each note declares, 'You are with me.'
In the silence, love takes flight,
A symphony of purest light.

With hands entwined, they pray as one,
Their hearts ablaze like the sun.
In sacred rhythm, they engage,
Writing love upon each page.

Through trials faced and joys embraced,
In every moment, love interlaced.
They sing of hope, they sing of peace,
In every song, their souls release.

The echoes rise like incense sweet,
In every heartbeat, love's retreat.
As ascendant love finds its way,
In songs of glory, they will stay.

The Light from Two Hearts

In the hush of dawn's embrace,
Two hearts gather in sacred space.
Their rhythms sync, a gentle beat,
In love's warmth, they feel complete.

Through shadows cast, their glow ignites,
A beacon bright in darkest nights.
With every word, a prayer is spun,
In the light, they become as one.

In silence shared, their souls converse,
A sacred bond that feels like verse.
With love, they build a world anew,
In harmony, their spirits grew.

As stars align and fate bestows,
In every glance, the spirit flows.
Together bound, they stand apart,
In the journey of the heart.

The light they share, a sacred flame,
In every moment, love remained.
Two hearts entwined in divine art,
Together, they cannot depart.

Reaching for the Divine in Each Other

In every gaze, a spark ignites,
Reaching for heaven, scaling heights.
In sacred whispers, truths align,
Two souls embraced, forever twine.

With every touch, the heavens hum,
In love's embrace, they overcome.
Hands clasped tight, they seek the skies,
In unity, their spirit flies.

They walk the path of sacred quest,
In each other's arms, they find rest.
Through trials faced and victories sought,
In love's embrace, the battles fought.

Together seeking, hearts aflame,
Inpassion's dance, they call His name.
With every heartbeat, they ascend,
Reaching for God, their souls extend.

In every prayer, a pledge is made,
As love's light never does fade.
In this journey—so divine,
Together, their hearts align.

Cherubic Harmonies

In realms where angels sing in grace,
Their voices weave a sacred space.
With wings of light they gently soar,
In praise of love forevermore.

With hearts aligned in thund'rous praise,
They dance along eternal ways.
In unity, their spirits gleam,
Awakening a holy dream.

The joy of heaven fills the air,
Each note a prayer, a soft affair.
They echo truths from ages past,
In every harmony amassed.

So let our souls like angels rise,
To seek the light beyond the skies.
In cherubic song let us abide,
With love and faith forever tied.

The symphony of grace unfolds,
In beauty that the heart beholds.
With each sweet sound, our souls ignite,
In cherubic harmonies of light.

The Path of Holy Union

Upon the way of truth we tread,
With sacred light our spirits fed.
In every step, the heart's intent,
With faith as guide, our souls are bent.

The whispers of the past remain,
In silent echo, love's refrain.
The sacred bond, a guiding flame,
In holy union, we proclaim.

Together on this hallowed ground,
In grace and mercy we are found.
Each prayer a step towards the sky,
In trust and love, we learn to fly.

Through trials faced and blessings shared,
In hearts awakened, souls declared.
The path to Him, forever clear,
In holy union, draw us near.

So let us walk, hand in hand,
In faith united, we shall stand.
With every heartbeat, ever one,
On this path, our journey spun.

Radiance of Affectionate Reverence

In the glow of morning's light,
We stand in awe, hearts shining bright.
With gratitude our spirits raise,
In radiant love, we sing His praise.

Each moment charged with His embrace,
We find our peace in every space.
In reverence deep, our hearts align,
With affection pure, His love divine.

The beauty of creation sings,
In fleeting joys and gentle things.
In nature's breath, we know His name,
In every heart, His love inflamed.

With humble hearts, we seek to know,
The depth of love that He will show.
In every prayer, a radiant beam,
An affectionate and holy dream.

Together, souls of light entwined,
In reverence's glow, forever bind.
In each embrace, the radiance flows,
Through paths of love, our spirit grows.

Embraced by the Celestial

In sacred light, we find our peace,
With every moment, fears release.
Embraced by grace, so soft and warm,
In celestial arms, we find our calm.

The heavens whisper sweetly low,
In gentle breezes, love will flow.
In starlit nights, our hearts take flight,
With every breath, we seek the light.

Together in the cosmic dance,
In faith and hope, we find our chance.
Each star a promise, love's decree,
Embraced by the celestial sea.

With arms outstretched, we rise above,
In joyful songs of boundless love.
In faith's embrace, we find the way,
To shine as stars in night's array.

So let us dance in radiant joy,
Where celestial light we shall employ.
In every heartbeat, pure delight,
Embraced by heavens, ever bright.

Ethereal Bridging of Souls

In the realm where spirits soar,
Love's whisper echoes evermore.
Threads of light, a sacred tie,
Binding hearts beneath the sky.

With every prayer that we weave,
Faith in each other we believe.
Stars above, bright guiding flames,
Call our souls by sacred names.

Through trials faced, we rise renewed,
In every tear, our hearts subdued.
The bridge we walk, a holy way,
Guiding us to break of day.

In silence shared, our spirits sing,
A harmony that angels bring.
With open arms and hearts unsealed,
A love divine is thus revealed.

Together we embrace the light,
In holy union, hearts take flight.
This ethereal dance, we find,
Transcendent bonds that ever bind.

The Sacred Dance of Beating Hearts

In twilight's glow, the heartbeat plays,
A sacred rhythm, love's sweet phrase.
Two souls entwined in gentle grace,
Through every glance, a warm embrace.

The dance of life, a holy swirl,
Where echoes of devotion curl.
Each step we take, together strong,
In harmony, where we belong.

With whispered vows, the night adorned,
Through every storm, our love reborn.
In sacred circles, we find peace,
As faith and trust in us increase.

The beating hearts, a symphony,
Resounding in eternity.
In every twirl, a glimpse above,
A testament of boundless love.

With souls aflame, we journey far,
Guided by an endless star.
In sacred dance, our spirits soar,
Connected forever, evermore.

Chasing the Dawn of Affection

When morning breaks and shadows fade,
Hope awakens in light displayed.
With open arms, we greet the day,
Chasing the dawn in our own way.

Through fields of gold, we run untamed,\nIn every
heartbeat, love is claimed.
With gentle whispers, winds will share,
Secrets of a love laid bare.

The sun rises, a sacred sight,
Illuminating hearts with light.
We chase the moment, pure and true,
Creating dreams anew, with you.

Each step we take, the path divine,
In every glance, your heart meets mine.
Together, we embrace the grace,
Of chasing love's most tender space.

As twilight comes, our spirits blend,
In every breath, on love we depend.
Chasing the dawn, forever free,
Bound by affection, you and me.

Illuminated Pathways of Togetherness

Through gardens rich, where blessings flow,
We walk together, hearts aglow.
Each step a promise, softly made,
On illuminated paths we wade.

With every word, a spark ignites,
Creating warmth on chilly nights.
In togetherness, our spirits shine,
A tapestry of love entwined.

Through valleys deep, our strength unfolds,
With faith unbroken, love upholds.
The light we share, a guiding star,
Illuminates our journey far.

In quiet moments, hand in hand,
We tread the earth, we make our stand.
With open hearts, we carve our way,
On pathways bright, come what may.

For in this life, we are the light,
Together, souls take joyous flight.
With every heartbeat, truth is found,
On illuminated paths, we're bound.

Faithful Ascent of Unified Souls

In valleys deep, where shadows dwell,
We seek the light, we hear the bell.
With hearts aligned, we climb the peak,
In faith's embrace, we find the meek.

Each step we take, a prayer we weave,
With every breath, our souls believe.
Together strong, hand in hand we go,
United in love, through pain and woe.

The clouds will part, the heavens sing,
As we ascend, our spirits wing.
In harmony, we rise above,
To realms unknown, we soar with love.

The stars will guide our faithful quest,
While sacred peace adorns our rest.
With trust as our anchor, we will thrive,
In the unity, our souls arrive.

So let us lift our voices high,
Together strong, we shall not die.
In faith we stand, our spirits whole,
Forever bound, one faithful soul.

Love's Ethereal Journey

In the silence, love takes flight,
It glows like stars, a guiding light.
Across the skies, our spirits soar,
In love's embrace, we seek for more.

With gentle grace, we walk this road,
Each step a promise, a sacred code.
Through trials faced and lessons learned,
In every heart, a fire burned.

The rivers flow, the meadows bloom,
In love's pure essence, we lose all gloom.
With eyes closed tight, we greet the dawn,
In every moment, our hearts are drawn.

Through storms and calm, we journey forth,
In every tear, we find new worth.
As shadows dance and light caress,
In love's sweet arms, we find our rest.

Beyond the realms of time and space,
In every heartbeat, we embrace.
With sacred vows, we weave our fate,
In love's embrace, we celebrate.

Embers of Divine Affection

In the quiet, embers glow,
A warmth within, a sacred flow.
Souls ignited, hearts entwined,
In divine love, we seek and find.

Each whispered prayer, a flame that sparks,
In shadows cast, we leave our marks.
Through trials faced, our spirits blend,
With every moment, we transcend.

In the light of truth, we stand so tall,
Each heartbeat echoes, love's sweet call.
Through endless nights, we hold the flame,
In divine affection, we find our name.

Together we rise, through joy and strife,
In every challenge, we find new life.
With every breath, our spirits soar,
In love's deep well, forevermore.

Embers dance in sacred night,
With gentle hands, we share our light.
In unity forged, our hearts are blessed,
In divine affection, we find our rest.

Vinculum of Sacred Hearts

In quiet moments, hearts entwine,
The sacred bond, a love divine.
With threads of gold, we weave the day,
In harmony, we find our way.

Through trials faced, our spirits rise,
In every laugh, a truth belies.
Together strong, we face the storm,
In faithful arms, we feel the warm.

As whispers float on gentle breeze,
In love's embrace, our souls find ease.
With every touch, a spark ignites,
In tender grace, we share our sights.

The moments shared, a timeless song,
In sacred love, we both belong.
With open hearts, we journey forth,
In a sacred bond, we find our worth.

So let us forge this sacred path,
In joy and love, we learn to laugh.
As one we stand, forever strong,
In our vinculum, we both belong.

The Ascending Spirit of Love

In the light of dawn, love rises,
Binding souls with gentle ties.
Through each heart, a flame ignites,
A celestial dance of sacred sights.

Grace descends from realms above,
Whispering softly, a hymn of love.
Unity flows like a river wide,
In the embrace of the Spirit, we abide.

As the stars twinkle in the deep,
In our hearts, the promise we keep.
Love ascends beyond all fear,
A guiding star, forever near.

With open hands, we raise the song,
In each note, we find where we belong.
Faithful hearts in joyous flight,
Together we soar, ignited by light.

In the silence, let love abide,
In every heart, our Savior's guide.
The spirit lifts, set free to roam,
In the love divine, we find our home.

Soul's Elevation in Sacred Song

In the quiet night, hearts sing,
Lifting spirits on angel's wing.
Melodies rise, a soft caress,
In each note, we find our blessedness.

Voices mingle, intertwine,
Every breath a step divine.
Harmony flows like water clear,
In sacred song, we shed our fear.

Each heartbeat echoes the divine,
In every silence, sacred signs.
With faith as our unwavering guide,
We journey forth, hearts open wide.

Through valleys low and mountains high,
Our souls resonate, we touch the sky.
In every lyric, hope is found,
The soul's elevation, sacred ground.

As we gather, hand in hand,
In this chorus, we will stand.
In love's embrace, we lift our tone,
The sacred song leads us home.

The Journey Beyond the Veil

Through the mist, a path unfolds,
Whispers of truth in stories told.
Beyond the veil, a light so bright,
Guiding souls through the long night.

Every heartbeat echoes the call,
To rise anew, to stand tall.
In the shadows, spirits gleam,
Navigating life, a sacred dream.

As we wander through the unknown,
In unity, we find our own.
With each step, the veil grows thin,
Awakening the divine within.

In the silence, we hear the song,
Of love eternal, where we belong.
On this journey, hand in hand,
Together we'll traverse this land.

At the journey's end, a light shall shine,
In every heart, the love divine.
Beyond the veil, we find our grace,
In the eternal, we embrace.

Divine Harmonies in Affection

In the quiet, a melody plays,
Divine harmonies through our days.
Affection blooms, a sacred art,
Uniting every beating heart.

Through laughter shared and tears we shed,
In every moment, love is bred.
Harmony weaves through trials faced,
In every challenge, God's embrace.

With open arms, we gather near,
Letting go of doubt and fear.
In every note, affection sings,
Propelling us on love's great wings.

Together we rise, unbroken, bold,
In the warmth of love, hearts unfold.
Divine grace pours like gentle rain,
In harmony, we find no pain.

With each sunrise, our spirits soar,
In divine affection, we explore.
Together we sing, a tender tune,
In love's embrace, we find our boon.

Ascending the Ladder of Affection

In the stillness of prayer, we rise,
Hearts entwined, reaching for the skies,
Each step a whisper, love's embrace,
Guiding us to our sacred place.

Through trials faced with grace divine,
We hold each other, your heart and mine,
With every ladder rung, we climb,
A rhythm of devotion, pure as time.

In unity, our spirits soar,
Together bound, forevermore,
With kindness lighting every path,
We share the joy, we share the laugh.

As we ascend, our burdens shed,
In love's bright light, our spirits fed,
Hand in hand, we journey on,
Towards horizons, a new dawn.

The ladder whispers, never cease,
In affection's rise, we find our peace,
Grateful hearts, in praise we sing,
For love, our faith, our everything.

Illuminated by Compassion

In the depths of night, a light breaks through,
A glow of hope, for me and you,
Compassion's touch, a gentle hand,
Guiding our hearts to understand.

Each tear shed speaks of love's embrace,
A sacred bond time can't erase,
In the soft glow, we find our way,
Through trials faced, in night and day.

With open hearts, we share the load,
Compassion's path, a sacred road,
Together we heal, side by side,
In love's warm glow, we will abide.

Illuminated by the light we find,
Healing whispers, hearts aligned,
In every act of kindness shown,
The seeds of grace are gently sown.

So let compassion be our guide,
In unity, we shall abide,
Together shining, never dim,
Illuminated, we are Him.

Elevated by Gentle Hearts

With gentle hearts, we rise each day,
In love's warm embrace, we find our way,
A soft touch speaks where words may fail,
In kindness shared, we shall prevail.

Through trials faced, our spirits lift,
With every act, we give a gift,
In harmony, our voices blend,
On gentle whispers, we depend.

Let compassion guide our every deed,
In the garden of love, we plant the seed,
As we nurture with care, hearts entwined,
In the grace of each other, peace we find.

Elevated high, above the fray,
Together in light, we choose to stay,
Through storms and trials, we stand strong,
With gentle hearts, we all belong.

So may our love be ever true,
In the quiet moments, just me and you,
Elevated by hearts that gently care,
In the sacred bond, a love we share.

The Sacred Fire of Connection

In the heart's core, a flame ignites,
A sacred fire, shining bright,
It warms the soul, it heals the pain,
In love's embrace, we break the chain.

Through storms of doubt, it fiercely burns,
In every heart, a lesson learns,
Connection deep, like roots entwined,
In the sacred fire, hope we find.

Together gathered, in unity we stand,
Holding space, a shining hand,
In the glow of love, we find our way,
The sacred fire guides each day.

Let passion flow, let hearts be free,
Bound by love, in harmony,
In the sacred fire, we come alive,
In every moment, we shall thrive.

So cherish the flame, tend it well,
In stories of love, we'll always dwell,
The sacred fire, our hearts collect,
In the warmth of connection, we reflect.

Ascension Through Kindred Spirits

In the light of dawn we rise,
With hearts entwined as one,
Through trials vast and skies,
Our journey has begun.

Together we ascend,
With faith our guide and grace,
In a bond that will not end,
We find our sacred place.

In whispers soft and clear,
The truths begin to flow,
Through love that draws us near,
The depths of spirit grow.

As stars align in night,
We reach beyond the veil,
With joy our souls take flight,
On wings of love we sail.

A circle forged in fire,
In unity we stand,
With hearts that never tire,
Together hand in hand.

Celestial Bonds

In twilight's gentle grace,
We gather 'neath the stars,
A tapestry we trace,
With love that heals our scars.

The heavens sing our song,
As spirits intertwine,
In harmony we belong,
In purpose, pure and divine.

With every breath we take,
We soar on sacred streams,
For love's own truth we make,
A bridge to share our dreams.

Through trials we abide,
In trust we shed our fears,
With every step beside,
Our hearts unlock the years.

The light within us glows,
A beacon through the night,
In celestial flows,
We rise to greater height.

Love's Sacred Voyage

Upon the waves of grace,
We sail to realms unknown,
With love we trim the lace,
In unity we've grown.

The compass of our hearts,
Guides us through the storm,
As magic starts and parts,
In each embrace, we warm.

In whispers of the wind,
Our dreams set forth to roam,
With faith our hearts rescind,
The fears that keep us home.

With trust as our anchor,
We venture forth in prayer,
Through every wave and fray,
Our souls beyond compare.

As dawn paints skies anew,
Our vessel finds its way,
In love we will pursue,
This sacred voyage stay.

Ascending Together in Spirit

In tranquil waters deep,
Our spirits start to rise,
With every promise keep,
We find the strongest ties.

As mountains touch the sky,
Our hearts begin to soar,
With faith that will not die,
We seek forevermore.

With every step we take,
A path is gently laid,
In love, no hearts will break,
For joy will never fade.

The stars align above,
To guide us on our quest,
In unity and love,
We find our truest rest.

Let each soul's light shine,
As we ascend with grace,
In faith, your hand in mine,
Together, we embrace.

Divine Light in the Darkness

In shadows deep, His light will guide,
A beacon bright, our hopes abide.
With whispers soft, He calms our fears,
In hearts of stone, He dries our tears.

As night may fall, His rays still shine,
A sacred warmth, a love divine.
Through darkest paths, His hand will lead,
In every heart, He plants the seed.

In trials fierce, our faith will grow,
Through every pain, His presence flows.
We walk not alone, but in His grace,
Eternally, in His embrace.

So let us raise our voices high,
In worship pure, we will not die.
For in the dark, His light will stay,
A guiding star, a golden ray.

Transcendent Affections

In silent prayer, our souls entwine,
Through whispered words, His love define.
With every heartbeat, draw us near,
In sacred moments, feel no fear.

The universe in Him abides,
In every age, His grace provides.
From mountain high to ocean wide,
In every heart, He will reside.

The warmth of love in every fold,
A truth that never grows too old.
He lifts us up, we soar above,
In holy light, we find our love.

Embrace the joy, let spirits rise,
In every tear, the sweet reprise.
Together bound, through faith we'll stand,
In unity, we'll hold His hand.

A Higher Calling of the Soul

Awake, dear heart, to purpose clear,
In every step, His voice we hear.
With open eyes, we seek the call,
As shadows fade, we rise and fall.

The journey wide, the path unknown,
In every trial, His mercy shown.
With faith as anchor, hope will soar,
In every breath, we'll seek the more.

The whispers hold a truth profound,
In every lost, a love is found.
Our souls aflame, ignited bright,
In essence pure, we chase the light.

In sacred trust, we move ahead,
By faith we walk, by grace we're led.
For in this calling, hearts unite,
In harmony, we share the light.

Wings of Grace

With wings of grace, we rise on high,
Embracing all, we touch the sky.
In gentle winds, His love will flow,
Through every trial, our spirits grow.

The burdens lift, our hearts set free,
In faith we soar, in harmony.
Through storms and strife, we find our peace,
In every prayer, the fears release.

With every step, He walks beside,
In trials fierce, we shall abide.
With open hearts to give and share,
In wings of love, we rise in prayer.

So let the world in shadows tread,
For we are led where angels thread.
In grace, we'll find our deeper song,
Together bound, forever strong.

Eternal Flame of the Heart

In silence deep, the heart does glow,
A flame divine, in sacred flow.
It lights the path, where shadows fall,
A beacon bright, it calls us all.

With every prayer, it burns so pure,
A promise kept, a love secured.
Through trials faced, it stands the test,
A gift of light, we are so blessed.

In stillness found, in faith we trust,
The flame ignites, sacred and just.
An endless spark, in darkest night,
Guiding our souls, towards the light.

Within the heart, each whisper sings,
Of hope and peace, the joy it brings.
For in its warmth, our spirits rise,
Eternal flame, our heart's delight.

So let it blaze, with fervent grace,
In every soul, in every place.
For as we love, we too shall see,
The flame of God, alive in me.

Graceful Ascent of Souls

In morning light, the spirits soar,
On wings of hope, forevermore.
Each step towards the heavens bright,
A graceful dance, in purest light.

Through trials faced, they find their way,
The guiding stars, in night and day.
With every breath, they rise anew,
In love and faith, their journey true.

The echoes call, from heights above,
In whispered winds, they speak of love.
A tapestry of hearts entwined,
In sacred bonds, they are defined.

With open arms, the heavens greet,
The souls that weave, life's tapestry sweet.
In unity, they find their song,
Together strong, where they belong.

So let us lift, our voices high,
In praise and thanks, to the sky.
For in this grace, our souls ascend,
To realms of peace, where life won't end.

Ascendance in Devotion

Amidst the storms, our hearts unite,
In steady hands, we seek the light.
Through every prayer, and every creed,
We rise as one, in sacred deed.

The journey long, the path unclear,
Yet in devotion, we draw near.
Together bound, in faith we strive,
In each other's love, we come alive.

With open hearts, we face the dawn,
In every sacrifice, a pledge reborn.
For each small act, our spirits grow,
In gentleness, the true love flows.

The sacred bond, of hope and grace,
In every trial, we find our place.
And as we toil, we are refined,
Ascendance found, in hearts aligned.

So let this devotion never fade,
In every moment, our lives displayed.
For as we rise, in love's embrace,
We find our truth, in this vast space.

Wings of Compassion

In tender care, the spirit glides,
On wings of love, where kindness abides.
With every act, a heart expands,
A gentle touch, from loving hands.

Through pain and sorrow, we break the chains,
With compassion's grace, we soothe the strains.
For every soul, deserves a chance,
To rise in joy, to find the dance.

With open hearts, we lend our ear,
To every voice, we hold so dear.
In unity, we share the weight,
Transforming lives, with love innate.

So let us spread our wings so wide,
In acts of kindness, let love reside.
For in each gesture, big or small,
We lift each other, and we stand tall.

As birds of peace, we soar above,
In a world united, filled with love.
For with each heartbeat, let it be
Wings of compassion, setting us free.

Celestial Apparitions of Boundless Love

In the heavens where angels soar,
A light descends, pure and sure.
Whispers of grace in the air,
Love eternal, beyond compare.

Each star a promise, a guiding sign,
Hearts entwined in a dance divine.
Infinite mercy shines so bright,
Comforting souls in the darkest night.

With every breath, we seek the way,
Casting our fears, come what may.
In unity, we rise above,
Embraced forever by boundless love.

Celestial hymns serenade the meek,
In their presence, our spirits speak.
Gathered together, we find our place,
Wrapped in warmth of divine grace.

Awake, arise, in faith we stand,
United in heart, hand in hand.
For in this life, through joy and pain,
Celestial love shall ever reign.

The Wake of Holy Union

From ashes rise the whispered vows,
In sacred circles, the spirit bows.
A bond transcends both time and space,
In quietude, we find our grace.

The coming together of souls entwined,
In every heartbeat, love defined.
With every moment, we create a song,
In holy union, we forever belong.

The light of dawn reveals the truth,
In spirit's embrace, we find our youth.
When paths converge in sacred trust,
Hearts awaken in divine gust.

Let joy resound through valleys low,
In this wake, let our spirits grow.
For in the union, we shall find,
The touch of God in every kind.

Eternal blessings gently flow,
Through trials faced, love shall glow.
In faith we move, a dance of grace,
In holy union, a warm embrace.

Spiritual Elevation of the Heart

In stillness soft, the heart takes flight,
Reaching higher into the light.
Each prayer a song, a tender plea,
Seeking solace, pure and free.

With every beat, a story told,
Of love divine, both brave and bold.
Lifted by hope, the soul ascends,
A journey shared with faithful friends.

In moments where the spirit swells,
Echoes of grace in sacred wells.
Through trials faced, we rise anew,
In the embrace of the ever true.

Let kindness flow like rivers wide,
In hearts aglow, we'll abide.
Together, as one, we seek the dawn,
The elevation of love, a sacred bond.

For in the heights where we reside,
No fear or doubt can now divide.
With hearts uplifted, we proclaim,
A spiritual elevation in His name.

Anointed Threads of Kindness

In every act of tender grace,
We weave the fabric of love's embrace.
Threads of kindness, bright and true,
Stitching hearts with colors anew.

A whisper shared, a helping hand,
In simple moments, together we stand.
With each gesture, the spirit ignites,
In unity formed, heartwarming sights.

Compassion flows like a river's stream,
In every touch, we build the dream.
With love anointed, we embrace the call,
To lift each other, together we fall.

Together, we sow the seeds of peace,
In shared laughter, our worries cease.
The joy of giving, the essence plain,
Anointed threads in love's sweet reign.

So let us walk, hand in hand,
In kindness' name, through this blessed land.
For in the warmth of every deed,
We find the truth of love's great need.

Seraphic Embrace of Unity

In the stillness, spirits soar,
Hand in hand, we seek the core.
Angels whisper songs of grace,
Binding souls in a sacred space.

Hearts aligned, a radiant glow,
Love unfurls, like flowers grow.
Unity's dance, a holy thread,
In harmony, our fears are shed.

Together we rise, as one we stand,
Guided gently by His hand.
With every prayer, our hopes entwine,
In seraphic embrace, divinely mine.

Through trials faced, we find our way,
In faith's light, we will not stray.
Each act of kindness, seeds we sow,
In the garden of love, forever flow.

As dawn breaks forth, a new refrain,
A chorus woven, beyond the pain.
In every heart, His love ignites,
In unity's glow, we reach new heights.

Celestial Chronicles of Affection

Beneath the stars, our souls entwine,
Each moment shared, a sacred sign.
In the silence, love's gentle ring,
Whispers of hope, eternally sing.

With every challenge, we grow strong,
In faith's embrace, we both belong.
Through trials faced, we find our muse,
A tapestry of love to choose.

Time flows onward, hearts in flight,
Guided by grace, we seek the light.
In every tear, a lesson learned,
In every joy, our spirits burned.

Celestial tales, a bond divine,
In every chapter, love's design.
Through storms and peace, we will endure,
In this sacred space, we are secure.

Together we weave a story vast,
In faith's embrace, our shadows cast.
With each heartbeat, a promise made,
In celestial love, we are displayed.

The Light of Transcendence

In the twilight's glow, we rise anew,
Casting shadows, embracing the view.
The light within, a guiding spark,
Illuminating pathways in the dark.

With lifted hearts, we reach the skies,
In every smile, the spirit flies.
Transcendence calls, a sweet refrain,
Through every joy, through every pain.

Faith leads the way, a beacon bright,
In love's embrace, we find our sight.
Through valleys low and mountains high,
We journey forth, our spirits fly.

In whispered prayers, we find our peace,
A bond unbroken, our love's release.
In sacred moments, lives converge,
The light of Transcendence, love's great surge.

With every dawn, we rise again,
In His warm embrace, our hearts remain.
Together we shine, a radiant blend,
In the light of love, we transcend.

Divine Harvest of Hearts

In fields of grace, our hearts do grow,
A divine harvest, love's sacred flow.
With every seed, a promise made,
In the soil of faith, hopes cascade.

Through seasons change, we tend the land,
Hands together, we take a stand.
In gentle whispers, love's rain falls,
Nurtured dreams within these walls.

The fruit of labor, sweet and pure,
A testament to love's allure.
In moments shared, our spirits rise,
In the divine harvest, truth complies.

Gathered together, we celebrate,
In unity's warmth, we elevate.
With every heart, a melody sings,
In the dance of life, each joy brings.

Eternal blessings in every part,
In this divine harvest, we impart.
Together we reap, in love's embrace,
In the garden of faith, a wondrous place.

Ascending Harmony in Devotion

In the quiet hush of prayer's embrace,
Hearts unite in a sacred space.
With hands uplifted, we seek the Light,
Transcending shadows, embracing delight.

Voices soar like angels in choir,
Filled with hope, ignited by fire.
Each whisper a promise, each song a pledge,
In harmony's echo, our spirits wed.

Fervor rises with every refrain,
Boundless love in a celestial chain.
Tears of joy wash worries away,
In devotion's embrace, we forever stay.

Together we journey, hand in hand,
Across the valleys of faith we stand.
With every heartbeat, passion we share,
Ascending in grace, beyond all despair.

In silent resolve, our spirits entwined,
Each step a whisper, beautifully designed.
The path illuminated, aglow with trust,
In love's pure essence, forever we must.

The Serene Sanctuary of Love's Light

Beneath the arch of heaven's grace,
We gather in this holy space.
Like petals opening to dawn's sweet glow,
Hearts awaken, love starts to flow.

In this sanctuary of whispers divine,
Silent prayers like sweetened wine.
A tapestry woven with threads of gold,
In the warmth of love, our souls unfold.

The stars above in quiet adoration,
Reflect the light of our dedication.
In every heartbeat, a promise we make,
For love's sweet journey, we shall undertake.

Bathed in tranquility, our spirits sing,
To the melody of peace, our voices ring.
With faith as our compass, we rise above,
In the serene haven of eternal love.

As the sun bids farewell, we stand aligned,
Together in purpose, our souls combined.
In the twilight's glow, we feel the might,
Of love's embrace, a radiant light.

Spirit's Ascent through Shared Grace

In the embrace of silent prayer,
We find the strength to cast our care.
With open hearts, we touch the skies,
In the realm where spirit flies.

Hand in hand, we voyage forth,
Seeking the treasures of love's true worth.
With every step, a bond appears,
A bridge of faith bridging all fears.

With grace as our guide, we journey high,
Eclipsing shadows, we reach the sky.
In the sacred dance of soul's delight,
We find our purpose, we unite.

The essence of kindness flows through our veins,
In each gentle moment, the love remains.
With spirits entwined, we climb the steep,
In the heights of compassion, our souls will leap.

Together we rise, in joy and grace,
In the warmth of the sun, we find our place.
The horizon beckons, inviting us near,
In the dance of the sacred, we conquer fear.

Embracing Heavenly Affection

In the stillness of night, love's light ascends,
Wraps us gently as the darkness bends.
In sacred whispers, time stands still,
In the heart's embrace, we find our will.

Every heartbeat, a tender refrain,
Like echoes of joy in the pouring rain.
With arms wide open, we gather near,
In affinity's glow, we conquer fear.

The stars above, our guardians bright,
Guide our spirits in love's pure sight.
As moonlight dances on waters deep,
We hold the promises that we keep.

In the language of love, no words need to flow,
For in each glance, deep feelings grow.
With grace like a river, our souls intertwine,
Embracing affection, divine and benign.

With each passing day, we cultivate trust,
In the garden of love, bloom flowers of lust.
Heavenly affection, a treasure so rare,
In the tapestry of life, we forever share.

Whispers of the Divine

In silence, the spirit calls,
Soft echoes of love enthrall.
Gentle light across the sea,
Guiding hearts to sanctity.

In shadows deep, His grace descends,
A balm for wounds, the heart transcends.
With every breath, a sacred sigh,
In faith, we learn to live and fly.

Through trials faced, we find our way,
With whispers bright on this new day.
In unity, we rise and stand,
Bound by love, divinely planned.

The stars align, the heavens weep,
In joy and sorrow, our spirits leap.
With every prayer, a bridge is built,
In trust, our burdens turn to wilt.

In the stillness, His voice we hear,
A promise held through every tear.
Through valleys low and mountains high,
With faith as wings, we reach the sky.

Hymn of the Heart's Ascent

Awake, O heart, to grace's call,
In every rise, in every fall.
The melody of hope does soar,
Inviting souls to seek and explore.

With every step, the path grows bright,
In darkest hour, He is our light.
Through shadows cast, the heart shall climb,
In sacred rhythm, transcending time.

The truest love, a gentle guide,
In every storm, we do abide.
With hands outstretched, in faith we meet,
As angels gather 'round our feet.

Each note we sing, a prayer we weave,
In harmony, we shall believe.
In gratitude, our voices rise,
To touch the stillness of the skies.

In joy and sorrow's sweet embrace,
We find in Him our resting place.
Together bound by love's ascent,
Our hearts, a hymn, forever spent.

Seraphic Embrace

In evening glow, the angels hum,
Their whispers soft, like distant drum.
With arms outstretched, they weave our fate,
A tapestry of love innate.

Through trials faced, we find our peace,
In every heartbeat, sweet release.
With seraphs near, we rise anew,
In gentle grace, our spirits grew.

Beneath the gaze of stars that shine,
Our hopes entwined with love divine.
In sacred silence, truth is found,
A holy pulse, a sacred sound.

Through every tear, a seed is sown,
In fields of faith, love's essence grown.
With every sigh, a prayer released,
In this embrace, we are increased.

In rapture's glow, we find our way,
Through golden dawn and twilight gray.
With seraphic love, we rise and soar,
In heavenly grace, forevermore.

Harmony of Heaven's Heart

Upon the dawn, a gentle song,
In every note, we all belong.
The whispers of the skies above,
Resound with grace, resplendent love.

In quiet moments, truth reveals,
The sacred bond that gently heals.
In unity, our spirits fly,
As hearts aligned reach to the sky.

Through life's vast sea, we sail as one,
In every heartbeat, love's begun.
With every breath, a promise made,
In harmony, we step unafraid.

In sacred spaces, light pours down,
Embracing souls, the lost, the found.
With every prayer, the heart awakes,
In quietude, the spirit shakes.

Together bound in faith and grace,
We dance beneath the Maker's face.
In every heartbeat, trust we weave,
In harmony, we do believe.

The Offering of Togetherness

In the quiet of the dawn, we gather near,
Hearts entwined, casting away all fear.
With hands lifted high, we share our prayer,
In unity, love blossoms everywhere.

A tapestry woven with threads of grace,
In the warmth of each smile, our spirits embrace.
Together we stand, steadfast and bold,
A circle unbroken, a story retold.

Through trials and joys, we forge our way,
In each moment of stillness, we learn to sway.
The strength of our bond, a radiant light,
Guiding us gently through the darkest night.

From mountains to valleys, we tread this earth,
In laughter and tears, we find our worth.
Each step we take, a sacred decree,
In the offering of togetherness, we are free.

Graceful Journeys of the Affectionate

On paths adorned with tender bliss,
We walk hand in hand, sealed with a kiss.
With every heartbeat, love's rhythm flows,
In gentle whispers, our connection grows.

Through shadows that dance in the fading light,
We cling to each other, banishing fright.
With every embrace, our spirits ascend,
In the grace of our journeys, we find a friend.

The sun paints our way with hues divine,
In laughter and peace, our souls entwine.
Each lesson learned, a gift sent from above,
In the journey of life, we celebrate love.

Through valleys of sorrow, we stand as one,
In joyous moments, our hearts feel the sun.
With every step taken, we honor our trust,
Graceful journeys bind us, as surely they must.

Illuminated by Sacred Unity

In the heart of the cosmos, a light shines bright,
Together we walk, through day and night.
With every heartbeat, sacred bonds align,
In love's embrace, the world is divine.

With minds open wide, and spirits so free,
We find in each other, our true destiny.
In harmony's dance, we let spirits soar,
Illuminated together, we seek to explore.

We gather like stars in the canvas of space,
In unity's glow, we find our place.
Each moment, each breath, a testament true,
In this sacred journey, I am one with you.

Through trials and triumphs, our love we'll weave,
In the fabric of life, we choose to believe.
With hearts intertwined in this glorious light,
Illuminated by togetherness, bold and bright.

The Altar of True Connection

Here at the altar where hearts are laid bare,
We offer our souls, a promise to care.
With eyes full of trust, we seek to behold,
The beauty of love, more precious than gold.

In silence we gather, each spirit aligned,
In the warmth of our bond, true solace we find.
With words softly spoken, we cast our prayers,
For strength in connection, in moments we share.

Through laughter and sorrow, our hearts intertwine,
In the sacred embrace, our shadows combine.
As offerings made, we rise and we fall,
In the altar of connection, we cherish it all.

With every heartbeat, our presence defined,
In the journey of love, we welcome the blind.
Together as one, through the storms we'll abide,
The altar of true connection, our hearts open wide.

The Blessing of Shared Spirits

In the glow of sacred light,
We gather as one, hearts bright.
Together we weave our dreams,
In love's embrace, hope redeems.

Through trials faced and joys we share,
In whispered prayers, we lay bare.
Hand in hand, souls entwined,
In unity, our strength we find.

With each step on this holy ground,
The echoes of grace all around.
Together, we rise, never fall,
In spirit's dance, we heed the call.

In the depths of night, we shine,
Illuminated by love divine.
Sharing burdens, lifting pain,
In harmony, we rise again.

A bond forged in trust and care,
Hearts connected, our spirits rare.
In each heartbeat, a story flows,
In faith's embrace, our journey grows.

Elevated Whispers of Grace

In the quietude of the morn,
We lift our voices, souls reborn.
With each whisper, a prayer takes flight,
Guided by love, pure and bright.

The clouds part to reveal our truth,
In the heart of each, resides our youth.
In every pause, a chance to see,
The grace that binds both you and me.

Through trials that may shadow our days,
We find solace in sacred ways.
Each moment shared, a gift divine,
In elevated grace, we shine.

Together we climb, spirits high,
Reaching for heavens, touching the sky.
In every heartbeat, a gentle bow,
To the wonders that bless us now.

The sun dips low, yet hope remains,
Each shared tear, love's gentle rains.
In whispers soft, the heavens sing,
Of the joyful hearts that faith can bring.

Faithful Hearts in Ascension

With faithful hearts, we rise anew,
In every prayer, a promise true.
Together bound by love's embrace,
We journey forth in holy grace.

Through valleys deep and mountains high,
With spirits bright, we touch the sky.
In every challenge, a lesson learned,
In faith, our blessed hearts are turned.

Side by side, we walk this path,
In laughter's song and gentle wrath.
With faithful hands, we nurture dreams,
In love's embrace, our hope redeems.

Each step in trust, our spirits soar,
In unity, we open the door.
To realms of peace, where love abides,
In faithful hearts, the truth resides.

In blessing's grace, we find our way,
In every dawn, a brand new day.
Together anchored, we shall rise,
In faithful hearts, our souls comprise.

Celestial Tapestry of Connection

In the fabric of time, threads entwine,
Celestial beings, our spirits align.
Each star a beacon, bright, that glows,
In the tapestry of love, it shows.

With each heartbeat, we weave our song,
In sacred circles, where we belong.
In whispers soft, the truth unfolds,
As stories shared become pure gold.

Through the night sky, we seek and find,
The eternal bond of heart and mind.
Ascending together, hand in hand,
In love's embrace, we understand.

In stillness, we gather, hearts ablaze,
In every gaze, our spirits praise.
A tapestry woven with light so bright,
Connecting us all, in love's pure sight.

In the dance of life, we find our place,
Each thread a gift, a testament of grace.
Together we rise, in divine reflection,
In this celestial tapestry of connection.

Harmonious Ascent of the Heart

In silence, whispers rise to grace,
The heart hears truth in sacred space.
Mountains echo prayers of light,
Guiding souls through the holy night.

Each step a song, each breath a prayer,
Love's gentle touch is everywhere.
From shadows deep to the sunlit skies,
A symphony of hope never dies.

With faith as wings, the spirit soars,
Boundless love that ever explores.
In unity, the heart transcends,
With every heartbeat, the journey bends.

Through trials faced, the soul expands,
Held gently in the sacred hands.
In every tear, a lesson learned,
A flame of love forever burned.

Together we rise, together we sing,
In the embrace of what love can bring.
As hearts align, the world transforms,
In harmonious ascent, our hearts confirm.

Pilgrimage of Love's True Path

In the garden where the lilies bloom,
We wander through the soft perfume.
With each step, our spirits merge,
On love's true path, we seek to surge.

The river flows with ancient grace,
Reflecting peace in every face.
With gentle hands, we share our fears,
And wash away the longing tears.

Mountains rise, a challenge found,
But with love's light, we stand our ground.
Faith grows deeper with every stride,
In this sacred journey, love's our guide.

Through valleys low and skies so wide,
We find the truth we cannot hide.
With open hearts, we learn to see,
The beauty of love that sets us free.

In unity, we walk this quest,
For in love's arms, we find our rest.
As souls entwine on love's true path,
In sacred moments, we share our laugh.

The Alchemy of Heart and Spirit

In the crucible of life, we blend,
Love and light, our truest friend.
With every heartbeat, magic stirs,
The alchemy of love occurs.

From ashes rise, the spirit gleams,
Transforming fear into our dreams.
Each moment blessed, a cherished gift,
In love's embrace, our souls uplift.

The essence glows in every heart,
Creating beauty through love's art.
In trials faced, we find our gold,
The stories of our souls unfold.

With open hands, we shape our fate,
In unity, we celebrate.
With every tear, a lesson learned,
In love's embrace, our spirits turned.

Together we weave the threads of light,
In the dance of joy, we take flight.
For in this alchemy, we find our part,
The sacred bond of heart to heart.

Souls Intertwined in Sacred Harmony

In gentle whispers, love's embrace,
Two souls unite in sacred space.
A dance of spirits, a melody sweet,
As hearts entwine, we find our beat.

In harmony's breath, we learn to trust,
Binding our dreams in love's pure dust.
With every gaze, a story told,
In sacred rhythms, life unfolds.

Through trials faced, together we stand,
In storms of life, we hold love's hand.
With every heartbeat, we're intertwined,
A sacred bond, divinely aligned.

In the silence shared, we find our song,
A symphony where we belong.
In moments still, our spirits soar,
Together as one, forevermore.

With every breath, we nurture light,
In the dance of love, our souls ignite.
In sacred harmony, forever we meet,
Two souls as one, in love's heartbeat.

The Symphony of Sacred Ties

In the hush of the dawn's bright light,
Voices rise in a hymn of delight.
Hearts entwined in a sacred refrain,
Echoing love like eternal rain.

Each note a prayer, each chord a bond,
In unity's dance, we feel so fond.
Guided by faith, our spirits soar,
Together we step through the open door.

In trials faced, our hands interlace,
Finding strength in this holy space.
Through shadows cast, we chase the light,
In the promise of grace, we take flight.

With each breath shared, a verse unfolds,
In the tapestry woven, a story told.
The rhythm of life, a sacred song,
In the heart's embrace, we belong.

So let us sing of the sacred ties,
In the symphony born, love never dies.
As we journey forth on this blessed path,
In delight we dance, escaping wrath.

Lattice of Divine Affection

Under the heavens, we weave our fate,
A tapestry bright, love's gentle state.
With threads of faith, we interlace,
In the lattice of affection, we find our place.

Each knot a promise, a bond so true,
In the warmth of the heart, love renews.
In the quiet moments, together we stand,
Embraced by the touch of a guiding hand.

Through trials faced and storms endured,
In this divine love, we are assured.
The lattice expands, with grace it grows,
In the light of truth, our spirit glows.

With whispers of hope, our dreams take flight,
In this sacred bond, we find our light.
With every heartbeat, a vow resounds,
In the lattice of love, eternity abounds.

So let us nurture this bond as one,
In the presence of grace, our fears are done.
Together we rise, in unity shine,
In the lattice of affection, divinely entwined.

The Prophecy of Eternal Togetherness

In shadows of night, we hear the call,
A prophecy whispered, uniting us all.
With love as our guide, we journey forth,
Toward the dawn's promise, a sacred worth.

Each step a testament, a vow to keep,
In the depths of faith, our souls shall leap.
Through valleys low and mountains high,
In togetherness, we learn to fly.

With hearts aligned, we travel as one,
Finding solace beneath the sun.
In every storm, our bond we test,
In the embrace of the divine, we rest.

The prophecy unfolds, a tale of grace,
In the harmony shared, we find our place.
With courage ignited, together we rise,
In the light of love, our spirit never dies.

So let us cherish this sacred vow,
In the depths of the heart, here and now.
Eternal togetherness, our guiding star,
In this journey of faith, we travel far.

Transfiguration through Shared Spirit

In the quiet moments, we find the spark,
A melding of souls, igniting the dark.
With shared spirit, our journey begins,
Transfiguration through love, the grace within.

As the sun sets, we gather as one,
In the warmth of connection, our fears undone.
With open hearts, we witness the light,
In each other's embrace, we take flight.

Through trials faced, we rise from the fall,
In the strength of our bond, we hear the call.
Together we flourish, each moment a gift,
In the shared spirit, our souls we uplift.

With every heartbeat, we echo the change,
Transfiguration unfolds, a beauty so strange.
In unity's light, we dance and we sing,
In the depths of our being, new life takes wing.

So let us rejoice in this love so rare,
In shared spirit's glow, we learn to care.
Together we rise, in faith we abide,
In transfiguration's grace, we forever reside.

Sacred Connections

In silence we gather, hearts intertwined,
A tapestry woven, by love so divine.
Each prayer a whisper, each breath a song,
In this sacred space, we truly belong.

Together we stand, in faith and in grace,
Shadows retreat in this heavenly place.
With kindness and mercy, our spirits unite,
Transforming the darkness, igniting the light.

In journeys of healing, we reach towards the skies,
With gratitude flowing, our souls will rise.
A bond that transcends what the eyes cannot see,
In the sacred connections, we find we are free.

Holding each other, like anchors of peace,
In love's gentle rhythm, our worries release.
Each moment a treasure, a gift from above,
In our sacred connections, we blossom in love.

Let faith be our beacon, as we walk hand in hand,
With trust as our compass, forever we stand.
In this sacred journey, we shine and we thrive,
For in every connection, our spirits revive.

Eternal Flame of Devotion

In the heart's quiet chamber, a flame burns so bright,
An eternal devotion, guiding through night.
With each tender moment, this love will endure,
An anchor of hope that remains ever pure.

Through trials and shadows, our spirits are tried,
With faith as our fortress, we stand side by side.
The warmth of this fire ignites every prayer,
In the depth of devotion, we find that we care.

In silence we listen, to whispers of grace,
The flame of our calling lights up every space.
Together we flourish, in God's loving gaze,
With hearts intertwined in a radiant blaze.

Through storms and distractions, we'll hold to this light,
For the eternal flame brings hope to our sight.
With love that's unending, just like a dream,
In this journey of faith, we rise and redeem.

With every new dawn, let our spirits align,
In the fire of devotion, your heart will be mine.
Eternal the promise, forever it stands,
In the flame of our love, we weave our own strands.

Luminescence of the Beloved

In the garden of stillness, your light starts to gleam,
A brilliance unyielding, like a sweet sacred dream.
Each whisper of presence, each gaze that we share,
In luminescence true, we are held in your care.

Transforming the shadows, your grace shines so clear,
With every soft gesture, I know you are near.
A beacon of warmth, in the depths of the night,
Your love is the compass that sets my soul right.

In the dance of existence, we twirl and we sway,
With laughter and joy, we brighten the day.
Your spirit a lantern, guiding each step,
In the luminescence of love, we are kept.

Together we wander through valleys and peaks,
In the light of the beloved, our soul language speaks.
With hearts wide open, the universe calls,
In this sacred embrace, through triumphs and falls.

Let the radiance of connection encompass our way,
For in every moment, love's light is the sway.
In this journey of faith, side by side we roam,
In the luminescence of love, we find our true home.

Spirit's Ascent in Togetherness

In the stillness of dawn, as the world starts to wake,
We rise in togetherness, for love's precious sake.
With hearts open wide, like the skies up above,
Our spirits ascend in the embrace of pure love.

Through valleys of trials, our bond will remain,
In the spirit of togetherness, we conquer the pain.
With hands intertwined, we journey through life,
Supported by each other through joy and through strife.

With whispers of kindness, we paint the divine,
In the fabric of life, our souls brightly shine.
Together we soar, transcending the grind,
In the spirit's ascent, on love we rely.

Amidst the great chaos, we find our sweet peace,
In the nurturing presence, all worries will cease.
For as one we awaken, to the song of the spheres,
In the resonance of love, we conquer our fears.

As we tread this path with hearts filled with grace,
In the spirit's ascent, love's beauty we trace.
Together forever, in God's gentle hand,
In this sacred togetherness, eternally we stand.

Ethereal Love's Elevation

In the quiet hush of night,
Heaven's whispers softly call.
Stars align in sacred light,
Creating bonds that never fall.

Hearts uplifted in pure grace,
Dancing in the cosmic flow.
In this vast, divine embrace,
Love's elevation starts to grow.

Angels sing with voices clear,
Guiding souls on sacred streams.
With each note, I feel you near,
Filling hearts with gentle dreams.

In the folds of time we weave,
Moments bright and full of peace.
In this love, we dare believe,
Eternal joy will never cease.

Together in the light we stand,
A tapestry of hope and trust.
Hand in hand, we walk the sand,
In love's embrace, we rise, we must.

Glorious Journeys of the Spirit

On winds of faith, our spirits soar,
Through valleys deep and mountains high.
With every step, we seek and explore,
In search of truth beneath the sky.

Guided by a flame that burns,
A light that never dims or fades.
With each lesson, the spirit learns,
As love within us gently wades.

The path we walk is paved in grace,
Each encounter a divine sign.
In every heart, we find a place,
Where loving kindness will entwine.

The spirit's journey knows no end,
For love will lead us through the night.
In every challenge, we transcend,
Finding solace in the light.

As we traverse this sacred ground,
Together, we embrace the call.
In unity, our hearts resound,
For glorious journeys are for all.

A Tapestry of Divine Affection

In the loom of grace, we intertwine,
Threads of love in colors bright.
Each moment shared, a sacred line,
Crafting beauty within the light.

With every heartbeat, souls unite,
Weaving dreams with trust and care.
In the silence, echoes ignite,
A divine embrace beyond compare.

Whispers of hope in the wind,
Stories told through gentle sighs.
Where love begins, we unpin,
Wings of faith which help us rise.

The fabric of our lives displays,
Miracles stitched in time's embrace.
In this tapestry, we praise,
The holy thread in every space.

Together we shall always stand,
In the light of God's connection.
Bound by love's eternal hand,
Creating our divine affection.

Bonds Beyond the Mortal

In the realm where spirits dwell,
Connections made in sacred trust.
Every soul a story to tell,
In love's embrace, we rise from dust.

Through trials faced and sorrows shared,
The bonds we forge, a force so strong.
In every heart, the love declared,
A melody to which we belong.

Beyond the veil, our hearts still dance,
In realms where love knows no bounds.
Taken by fate's tender chance,
In unity, our truth resounds.

Together we shall rise and soar,
In a light that guides our way.
With every whisper, we implore,
For bonds of love that never sway.

For in the end, what matters most,
Are the ties that cannot break.
In love's embrace, we find the boast,
That beyond the mortal, we awake.

The Sacred Dance of Two

In the stillness, they stand,
Hearts entwined, hand in hand.
A rhythm crafted by the divine,
In every step, love's design.

Circling under the watchful skies,
With whispers sweet, the spirit flies.
In the dance, two souls are one,
A sacred embrace, never to shun.

Seasons change, yet they remain,
Through joy and sorrow, loss and gain.
With grace they sway, time stands still,
In harmony, they bend to will.

As dawn unfolds with golden hue,
In every breath, life feels anew.
In the passion of the sacred light,
They find their way, through darkest night.

Together they rise, shining bright,
Reflecting love in celestial light.
In unity, the world they see,
A sacred dance, forever free.

Celestial Chords of Togetherness

In the quiet, a melody flows,
Hearts attuned as the spirit knows.
With every note, a prayer is spun,
Together they blossom, two as one.

Celestial chords, woven tight,
Echoing softly in the quiet night.
In harmony, their voices blend,
A resonant journey, without end.

Through valleys deep and mountains high,
Together they seek, together they try.
In every challenge, strength they find,
Two souls bonded, eternally aligned.

With grace they rise, touching the sky,
In every embrace, they silently sigh.
In the unity of love's sweet song,
They find their way, where they belong.

Whispers of hope, a guiding star,
No distance can sever, no pain can mar.
In the symphony of sacred grace,
Together they walk, their rightful place.

From Earth to Heaven

With heads bowed low, hearts uplift,
In every moment, a sacred gift.
From earthly bonds, they rise anew,
Together reaching, skies of blue.

Footprints marked on soil so dear,
Gentle reminders that love draws near.
With every prayer, they climb the way,
From shadows deep to light of day.

As dawn's embrace ignites the morn,
In cherished bonds, their souls are sworn.
Together they venture, hand in hand,
From fragile roots to promised land.

With whispered words, they touch the sky,
An ascension born from love's reply.
Through trials fierce, they find their might,
From earth to heaven, they take flight.

Together they sing in cosmic dance,
Grateful for every fleeting chance.
In the grace of love, they soar above,
From earth to heaven, bound by love.

The Grace of Mutual Ascent

As sunlight breaks, they rise as one,
In the journey where life's begun.
A path of trust, a sacred quest,
In mutual ascent, they find their rest.

With every step, they weave a thread,
In silent vows, their hearts are fed.
Ascending mountains, hand in hand,
Together strong, they make their stand.

Through valleys deep and shadows long,
In the grace of love, they grow strong.
With faith as their guide, they tread the way,
In unity's glow, they will not sway.

In whispered prayers, they find their voice,
In each other's strength, they rejoice.
Soaring high on wings of grace,
They seek the light in every place.

The beauty found in two as one,
In every dawn, a new day's sun.
In mutual ascent through all that's true,
Together they shine, forever renewed.

A Tapestry Woven by Devotion

In quiet halls where whispers soar,
The threads of faith unite and pour.
We weave our hope in sacred light,
Each prayer a spark in endless night.

Through trials faced, we find our way,
With hearts aflame, we kneel and pray.
Divine hands guide our steady course,
In love's embrace, we find our source.

With every stitch, a story told,
Of grace and mercy, strong and bold.
In unity, our spirits rise,
Together bound beneath the skies.

Within the fabric of our trust,
We gather strength, as we must.
In devotion's name, we shall not fall,
For love weaves through the hearts of all.

A tapestry, bright and divine,
In its pattern, our lives entwine.
Through every thread of sacred art,
We cherish the gifts of the faithful heart.

Reverence in the Journey of Hearts

In the temple of the soul, we stand,
With reverence shared, and faith unplanned.
Each journey marked by kindness's grace,
A sacred path in life's embrace.

With every tear and every smile,
We walk together, mile by mile.
In shadows cast and sunlight bright,
We find our way towards the light.

Our hearts unshaken, strong and free,
In unity, we find the key.
Divine whispers guide our way,
Through night's embrace, towards the day.

In love's vast ocean, we will sail,
With faith our compass, we shall prevail.
Through storms that rage and winds that wail,
In harmony, we shall not fail.

Holding hands in sacred trust,
We find the strength that's born from dust.
With every beat, our spirits sing,
In reverence, we embrace the spring.

Ascendancy of the Heart

With every breath, we rise, we soar,
In love's embrace, we seek for more.
The heart's ascent is pure and true,
In sacred love, we learn anew.

In faith's ascent, we shed our fears,
Each prayer uplifted through the years.
With gentle hands, the Spirit steers,
To heights where joy and grace appears.

In silence deep, our souls ignite,
With every thought, we merge with light.
Through trials faced, our courage grows,
In unity, our spirit flows.

With hearts prepared, we find our wings,
In sacred songs, our freedom sings.
As we ascend on love's great tide,
A journey blessed, with God as guide.

In every heartbeat, truth revealed,
A tapestry of love unsealed.
With open hearts, we reach the sky,
In trust, we rise, in faith, we fly.

Celestial Embrace

In twilight's warmth, the heavens glow,
A celestial dance, where spirits flow.
With every star, a whispered prayer,
In the night sky, we find our care.

Each heartbeat echoes in the night,
A melody of purest light.
With faith encased in divine grace,
We feel the touch of love's embrace.

In silence deep, we hear the call,
Of angels soaring, one and all.
Their wings enfold us, soft and true,
In each embrace, our hearts renew.

With every sigh, we touch the realms,
Where love materializes and overwhelms.
In celestial glow, our courage thrives,
In unity, the spirit strives.

In dreams we share, the heavens bend,
With faith, our souls shall never end.
In every heartbeat, we find grace,
In the boundless, we embrace our place.

The Holy Union of Kindred Spirits

In sacred space, our hearts align,
Beneath the stars, our souls entwine.
A bond divine, through trials we stand,
In faith and love, hand in hand.

Together we rise, like morning light,
Illuminated paths, a pure delight.
In kindness shared, our spirits soar,
An echo of grace, forevermore.

Each whispered prayer, a gentle call,
United we flourish, divided we fall.
With open hearts, we seek to know,
The strength of love in every glow.

In holy silence, wisdom grows,
Through trials faced, true love bestows.
In kindred spirits, we find our way,
A sacred promise, come what may.

Together we weave, a tapestry bright,
Threads of compassion, a wondrous sight.
In the union of hearts, we find our peace,
A journey of love that will never cease.

Sacred Waters of Nurtured Bonds

In gentle streams, our spirits flow,
The sacred bond we come to know.
With every ripple, a story told,
Of love and faith that never grow old.

In tranquil pools, reflection gleams,
Our hearts embrace like vibrant dreams.
Through storms and trials, we stand tall,
In sacred waters, we rise, we call.

The current strong, yet tender too,
In harmony's song, we find what's true.
With every drop, a promise made,
In nurturing love, our fears allayed.

We gather near, where spirits meet,
In unity found, our hearts repeat.
The sacred waters, pure as light,
Guide us through the darkest night.

Together we flow, forever bound,
In this sacred dance, our joy profound.
With open hearts, we drink the whole,
From sacred waters that nourish the soul.

Luminescent Threads of Belonging

In twilight's glow, we gather close,
Luminescent threads, our hearts engross.
Each truth we share, a shining spark,
A tapestry woven from love's own arc.

With every stitch, a story sewn,
In unity bright, together we've grown.
Across the miles, through time and space,
Our threads connect, a warm embrace.

As stars above, in silence shine,
We find our strength, our souls align.
In shared laughter, and tears we find,
The sacred bond that forever binds.

Each moment cherished, a thread refined,
In love's great loom, we're intertwined.
Through trials faced, our hearts thus bold,
In luminescent threads, our tale is told.

In harmony's glow, we see the light,
In every spirit, a sacred sight.
Connected as one, with hands extended,
In the dance of love, we are mended.

The Prayer of Intertwined Souls

In whispered prayer, our souls unite,
A sacred bond, a guiding light.
With every breath, we seek the divine,
In intertwined paths, our hearts align.

In sacred silence, our spirits soar,
Each moment shared, we yearn for more.
Through shadows passed, our voices rise,
In humble worship, we touch the skies.

Together we stand, as one we plead,
To nurture love, to plant the seed.
In every tear, a lesson learned,
In fervent faith, our hearts will burn.

With open arms, we greet the dawn,
In prayerful songs, we find our bond.
Though paths may twist, and trials come,
In sacred union, we overcome.

In every heartbeat, our love declared,
In whispered prayers, we are ensnared.
With intertwined souls, we face the day,
In love eternally, we find our way.

Celestial Silhouettes of Togetherness

In realms where shadows gently sway,
Two souls entwined, in light's soft play.
A bond unbroken, through time's embrace,
Together we shine, in sacred space.

With whispers sweet as morning's dew,
Hand in hand, our hearts renew.
Guided by stars, we rise above,
Celestial silhouettes of love.

In prayerful unity, we find our song,
A melody pure where we belong.
In faith and grace, our spirits soar,
Together forever, forevermore.

Through trials faced, we stand as one,
In the tapestry of life, our thread is spun.
With every heartbeat, our spirits weave,
A testament to love, we believe.

So let the heavens witness our truth,
In the dance of time, we claim our youth.
For in this journey, hand in hand we sing,
Celestial silhouettes, our offering.

The Altar of Everlasting Connection

Upon the altar, we gather near,
With hearts ablaze, embracing the clear.
In sacred silence, love's truth unfolds,
A bond unyielding, eternally holds.

With every promise, we seal the fate,
In divine essence, we elevate.
Connected souls in an endless strive,
The altar of love, where hope will thrive.

In gentle whispers, our vows proclaimed,
Each word a treasure, forever named.
Through trials faced, our love will shine,
An everlasting connection, divine.

With faith as our compass, we shall not stray,
Together guided, come what may.
In the warmth of grace, our spirits ignite,
At the altar of love, forever bright.

So here we stand, in endless prayer,
In joyful union, we shall declare.
For in our hearts, a sanctuary known,
The altar of connection, our love has grown.

Resplendent Harmonies of Divine Kinship

In the symphony of life, we merge our song,
Resplendent harmonies where we belong.
Each note a blessing, each chord a sign,
In divine kinship, our souls align.

With laughter's echo, our spirits dance,
In every glance, a sacred trance.
Together we soar, on wings of grace,
Resplendent harmonies in love's embrace.

Through trials faced, we find our way,
In the light of hope, we choose to stay.
Each heartbeat a rhythm, a shared decree,
In the tapestry of love, we are free.

With open hearts, we share our dreams,
In flowing rivers, love brightly beams.
We are the music, the soul's refrain,
Resplendent harmonies, a sacred gain.

As shadows fade, our light expands,
In divine kinship, we take a stand.
Together forever, through joy and strife,
In resplendent chords, we celebrate life.

Enlightened Steps on Love's Path

With every step, we walk in light,
Enlightened souls, hearts burning bright.
On love's path, we tread with grace,
In unity's warmth, our fears erase.

Through valleys low, and mountains high,
In love's embrace, we learn to fly.
With hands held tight, we face each day,
Enlightened steps, guiding our way.

In moments fragile, we find our strength,
Together we grow, in love's full length.
With open hearts, we share the load,
On love's path, we walk the road.

Each footprint left, a story told,
Of dreams fulfilled and hearts of gold.
In harmony's grace, we dance and sing,
Enlightened steps, our spirits cling.

So let us journey, hand in hand,
In love's embrace, we understand.
With every breath, together we'll chart,
Enlightened steps, forever in heart.

Radiant Union of Twin Flames

In celestial light, we unite,
Two souls woven close,
A dance of fire, pure and bright,
Our hearts' shared heartbeat boasts.

Every glance, a sacred grace,
Reflecting love's embrace,
In the vast, eternal space,
Together, we find our place.

From shadows, we rise anew,
Embracing joy and pain,
In every trial, love shines through,
Our spirits intertwined remain.

With divine whispers as our guide,
We journey hand in hand,
In faith and hope, we shall abide,
In this holy, promised land.

Through storms and calm, we soar high,
A union blessed by fate,
In the heavens, we will fly,
Twin flames, we celebrate.

Divine Elevation through Union

In harmony, we join as one,
Hearts aligned in sacred song,
With every breath, our spirits run,
Together, we are strong.

In the glow of love's pure light,
We ascend beyond all doubt,
In faith, we reach our greatest height,
Within, a holy shout.

The threads of destiny entwined,
In unity, we rise,
In every moment, love defined,
Our souls begin to fly.

As prayers weave through night and day,
A tapestry of grace,
In divine union, we shall stay,
In love's celestial embrace.

No fear can break this bond so true,
We'll rise above the storm,
In every dawn, our love renew,
Transcending every form.

The Promise of Ascendant Love

In whispers soft, we make a vow,
Our hearts, like stars, align,
With every breath, a sacred now,
In love's sweet, perfect sign.

Through trials faced, we stand as one,
Our spirits brightly shine,
In unity, let hope be spun,
In love's design divine.

As mountains bow and rivers bend,
So too, our souls will soar,
In each embrace, a timeless blend,
Promising forevermore.

With hands held tight, we'll brave the night,
Awakening the dawn,
In every choice, the path feels right,
Our love, the utmost bond.

In heavenly realms, we take our flight,
Beyond what eyes can see,
Together, crafting pure delight,
In love's eternity.

Touching the Divine Through Each Other

In quiet moments, we find peace,
A touch that stirs the soul,
As love blooms bright, our fears release,
Together, we feel whole.

In every heartbeat, grace unfolds,
A connection deep and pure,
In each story, love retold,
Our spirits shall endure.

Through trials faced and shadows cast,
In unity, we stand,
In every storm, our love holds fast,
Together, hand in hand.

In sacred silence, we align,
Reaching for the divine,
In every glance, a sacred sign,
In this love, we shine.

For in each other, hope ignites,
A flame that will not cease,
Through every day and sleepless night,
We find our perfect peace.

Unfolding the Heart's Sacred Potential

In silence, whispers of truth arise,
Tender grace wrapped in celestial ties.
Hearts awaken to a vibrant call,
In the stillness, we are one and all.

With each breath, divine love we share,
Unfolding the gifts laid lovingly bare.
A journey inward, sacred and bright,
Illuminating the path of pure light.

In prayerful moments, souls intertwine,
The essence of purpose, a holy design.
United, we stand, a compassionate choir,
Fanned by the flames of faith's sacred fire.

In the garden of hope, flowers bloom,
Each petal a promise, dispelling the gloom.
As we gather in love's warm embrace,
The heart's sacred potential finds its place.

Let forgiveness and mercy pave the way,
Transforming our hearts with each passing day.
Together, we rise, hand in hand,
In the unfolding of dreams, forever we stand.

In the Light of Togetherness

In the dawn, where shadows fade,
Unity blossoms, our spirits laid.
Each heart beats with a gentle song,
In the light of togetherness, we belong.

Through trials faced, we hold steadfast,
In love's embrace, our sorrows surpassed.
Together, we weave a tapestry bright,
Illuminated by faith's guiding light.

Voices lifted in harmonious prayer,
A symphony of hope, beyond compare.
In every moment, grace does abound,
In the light of togetherness, we are found.

Glimmers of kindness in each soul's gaze,
Awakening joy in countless ways.
With open hearts, let love be our guide,
In the bonds of togetherness, we abide.

Each step we take, a dance of the free,
In the sacred realm of unity.
Together we shine, an eternal flame,
In the light of togetherness, we proclaim.

Union of Graceful Souls

In sacred circles, we gather near,
Hearts aligned, shedding doubt and fear.
With grace as our anchor, hope our song,
In the union of souls, we are strong.

Through trials faced, we learn to rise,
In each other's arms, the love that ties.
A bond unbroken, divine and true,
In the union of graceful souls, we renew.

With gentle whispers, wisdom flows,
In shared connection, our essence grows.
Embracing the diverse, the unique we hold,
In the tapestry woven, our spirits unfold.

Let compassion be the bridge we build,
Hearts opened wide, with kindness filled.
In the sacred dance, we joyfully sway,
In the union of graceful souls, we pray.

With gratitude, we lift our praise,
In moments cherished through all our days.
Together we walk on this sacred road,
In the union of souls, love is bestowed.

The Ascent to Holy Connection

In the mountains high, where spirit soars,
We climb together, opening doors.
Each step a prayer, each breath a song,
In the ascent to connection, we belong.

Through valleys deep, we traverse as one,
With hearts ignited, we harness the sun.
In sacred silence, we find our way,
In the ascent to holy connection, we stay.

Hands intertwined, a journey embraced,
In the warmth of companionship, fears are faced.
Each shared smile, a beacon of light,
In the ascent to connection, love ignites.

With every heartbeat, the divine we seek,
In whispered truths, our souls do speak.
Boundless and free, we rise above,
In the ascent to holy connection, pure love.

Let gratitude flow in the mountains we tread,
As we wander on paths where angels have led.
In the embrace of the sacred, we are whole,
In the ascent to connection, united in soul.

9 789916 897522